STARS OF PRO WRESTLING

SHAWN MICHAELS

BY TIM O'SHEI

Consultant:
Mike Johnson, Writer
PWInsider.com

CAPSTONE PRESS
a capstone imprint

Edge Books are published by Capstone Press,
151 Good Counsel Drive, P.O. Box 669, Mankato, Minnesota 56002.
www.capstonepress.com
Copyright © 2010 by Capstone Press, a Capstone imprint.

092009
005619WZS10

Books published by Capstone Press are manufactured with paper
containing at least 10 percent post-consumer waste.

Library of Congress Cataloging-in-Publication Data
O'Shei, Tim.
    Shawn Michaels / by Tim O'Shei.
    p. cm. — (Edge books. Stars of pro wrestling)
    Includes bibliographical references and index.
    Summary: "Describes the life and career of pro wrestler Shawn
Michaels" — Provided by publisher.
    ISBN 978-1-4296-3947-7 (library binding)
    1. Michaels, Shawn. 2. Wrestlers — United States — Biography. I. Title.
II. Series.
GV1196.M53S43 2010
    796.812092 — dc22   2009027263

Editorial Credits
Kathryn Clay, editor; Kyle Grenz, designer; Jo Miller, media researcher;
    Laura Manthe, production specialist

Photo Credits
AP Images/Victoria Arocho, 23; CORBIS/Duomo, 24; Steven E. Sutton, 16
Getty Images Inc./AFP/John Mottern, 12; Russell Turiak, 17; WireImage for
    Lionsgate/John Sciulli, 29
Globe Photos, 11, 20; Graham Whitby-Boot/Allstar, 19
Newscom, cover, 5, 26; DoD photo by Lance Cpl Ruben D. Calderon, 27;
    Olivier Andrivon, 7; Splash News and Pictures/Doug Meszler, 9
Shutterstock/Chad Palmer, 15

Design Elements
Shutterstock/amlet; Henning Janos; J. Danny; kzww

TABLE OF CONTENTS

Chapter 1

WINNING THE CHAMPIONSHIP

One hour.

That's a long time to wrestle. Most professional wrestling matches last less than 20 minutes. Hardly any wrestling match takes a full 60 minutes — except this one.

It was March 1996, and this match was part of WrestleMania, pro wrestling's biggest event. Shawn Michaels, known as "The Heartbreak Kid," was getting his world title shot against Bret "Hit Man" Hart. Shawn had spent more than 10 years fighting for this chance. But the rules were different. This was an Iron Man match. Shawn and Hart would wrestle for an hour. The new world champion would be the man with the most pins. But would Shawn be able to last that long?

Shawn has wrestled in more than 15 WrestleMania matches.

Winning the World Championship title would not be easy. Shawn battled Hart as fans around the world watched. The wrestlers hit and kicked and twisted. But neither man fell to the mat.

As the clock wound down to zero, Hart locked Shawn in a *sharpshooter*. But Shawn never gave up. When time ended, it was announced that the match would go into overtime. The winner would be decided by sudden death. The first time a man was pinned, the match would be over. About two minutes into overtime, Shawn struck Hart with *Sweet Chin Music*, his **signature move**. Then he hit Hart with another. Hart wobbled and fell to the mat. Shawn covered him, ending the match. Shawn was now the world champion.

signature move — the move for which a wrestler is best known

WRESTLING MOVE

sharpshooter — when an opponent is on his back, the wrestler crosses the opponent's legs, flips him onto his stomach, leans back, and pulls up on the opponent's legs

Sweet Chin Music — a wrestler kicks an opponent in the chin with the sole of his foot

Shawn used Sweet Chin Music to defeat opponents such as Randy Orton.

Chapter 2

PROVING HIMSELF

Shawn Michaels was small for a wrestler. Many people thought he wouldn't make it. But he proved them wrong. Later, after leaving wrestling for four years, Shawn decided to come back. Again, people wondered if he could make it. And again, he proved that he could.

Proving himself has never been a problem. It's something he's had to do since birth. Shawn was born on July 22, 1965, in Chandler, Arizona. His real name is Michael Shawn Hickenbottom, but he likes to be called Shawn. His parents, Carol and Dick, already had two sons and a daughter.

When Shawn was born, Carol was disappointed. She had been hoping for a second daughter. At first, Carol didn't even want to see her son. The nurses at the hospital had to convince her to hold him. Once she did, Carol quickly fell in love with her new baby boy.

Shawn has worked hard to become a WWE superstar.

GROWING UP

Shawn's dad was in the military, which meant the family moved around a lot. Shawn lived everywhere from Arizona to England. Most of his childhood was spent in San Antonio, Texas. Shawn played baseball and basketball. In high school, he played football as an offensive lineman and a linebacker.

Shawn's interest in professional wrestling dates back to seventh grade. That's when he started watching wrestling on TV every Saturday. He read wrestling magazines and stood in front of mirrors while imitating his favorite champion, Ric Flair. Shawn practiced his wrestling moves with his friend Kenny Kent. Shawn and Kenny bodyslammed each other into swimming pools. The boys often went to wrestling matches together.

"Nature Boy" Ric Flair was a professional wrestler for 36 years. He retired in 2008.

Shawn was hit by Mike Tyson at WrestleMania XIV.

PURSUING A DREAM

After high school, Shawn went to college. He attended classes for about a year but didn't really like it. Shawn felt like college wasn't the right fit for him. He told his father he wanted to become a wrestler. Shawn had dreamed of becoming a professional wrestler since he was 12 years old. At age 19, Shawn was ready to pursue his dream. Dick wasn't sure this was a good choice. But he eventually gave in and supported Shawn. He even helped Shawn get started. Dick spoke to a family friend who knew a wrestling **promoter**. The promoter suggested Shawn enter a wrestling school.

Shawn was trained by José Lothario. For a $3,000 fee, he taught Shawn how to bodyslam and perform other wrestling moves. Shawn also learned how to safely fall and take blows.

promoter — someone who helps with the growth or development of a wrestler's career

ENTERING THE RING

After training for a few months, Shawn began competing. He wrestled in small shows in the southern and central United States. Then he landed a job competing at bigger shows in Texas. There, Shawn was a skilled **tag team** wrestler. He and partner Paul Diamond even won a championship.

MOVING UP

After eight months in Texas, Shawn joined the American Wrestling Association (AWA). He formed a tag team called the Midnight Rockers with Marty Jannetty. Both men were athletic. They could leap and spin while attacking opponents. They thought alike too. Each seemed to always know what the other was thinking.

tag team — when two wrestlers partner together against other teams

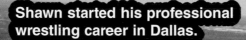

Shawn started his professional wrestling career in Dallas.

The pair spent most of 1986 chasing after another tag team made up of Doug Somers and Buddy Rose. They lost match after match until one day in January 1987. That's when Shawn and Marty finally defeated the Somers-Rose team and won the AWA World Tag Team belts. They held the championship title for four months. After losing it, they regained the belts at the end of the year.

The Midnight Rockers were one of the best tag teams in the AWA. But the pair was hoping for more. Shawn and Marty wanted to wrestle in the World Wrestling Federation (WWF), which is now called World Wrestling Entertainment (WWE).

WWE owner Vince McMahon hired Shawn in 1988.

The Belt That Never Was

Can a championship be won and then erased? It can if it's in professional wrestling.

In 1990, the Rockers squared off against the Hart Foundation for the championship title. The Rockers beat tag team champions Brett Hart and Jim Neidhart, but there was a problem. The top rope of the ring had broken. The broken rope limited the wrestlers' moves. It also cut down on the excitement. Though the match had been filmed, Vince McMahon didn't want to broadcast it. A broken-rope match wouldn't look exciting on TV. The results of the match were erased, and the Harts remained the champions.

Early in his career, Shawn faced off against Brett Hart.

Chapter 3

HEARTBREAKER

Shawn and Marty's success in AWA prompted Vince McMahon to hire them in 1988. With high-flying leaps and double *dropkicks*, Shawn and Marty pumped up the crowds. The pair came up with new moves and even used toy wrestlers to practice the moves. Shawn and Marty kicked, flipped, and bodyslammed the toys. Then the pair tried out the moves they liked. If the moves worked, they used them in the ring.

The Rockers stayed together in the WWF for four years. They **feuded** with famous tag teams Demolition, the Brainbusters, and the Hart Foundation. Despite the Rockers' popularity, Shawn wanted to wrestle solo. In early 1992, a TV interview set up between the pair turned into an argument. Shawn smashed Marty through a window. With that, Shawn was on his own.

feud — to argue and fight with another person or group of people

Shawn is known for his
signature pose in the ring.

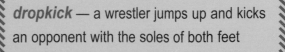

WRESTLING MOVE

dropkick — a wrestler jumps up and kicks
an opponent with the soles of both feet

Shawn lost a championship belt to Razor Ramon.

THE HEARTBREAK KID

Throughout his career, Shawn has been both a **babyface** and a **heel**. But when his singles career began in the early 1990s, Shawn was definitely a heel. With big muscles and long brown hair, he was loud and rude. He acted cooler than everyone around him. He did this to get noticed, and it worked. Shawn became known as "The Heartbreak Kid" — a good-looking guy who wasn't always nice.

babyface — a wrestler who acts as a hero in the ring

heel — a wrestler who acts as a villain in the ring

Intercontinental Champion

In October 1992, Shawn defeated "The British Bulldog" Davey Boy Smith to win the Intercontinental Championship. This was Shawn's first solo belt. It meant he was now a star. But he was also a target for other wrestlers who wanted his title. One of those wrestlers was his former partner, Marty Jannetty. The pair feuded for months.

In 1993, personal issues kept Shawn out of the ring for six weeks. WWE officials told Shawn to return the belt, but he refused. The WWE held a match to pick a new Intercontinental Champion. Wrestler Razor Ramon won the new belt. But when Shawn returned to the ring, he claimed he was still the champion. After all, he still had the belt that he had refused to give back.

So who was the true champion? The question would be settled with a ladder match. Shawn's old belt and Ramon's new belt dangled on a cable over the ring. The first wrestler to climb the ladder and grab the belts would claim the championship.

Ramon won that battle and the belts. But Shawn wasn't finished. He had more title matches in his future.

Chapter 4

FINDING HIS SMILE

In the two years following his championship win at WrestleMania, Shawn lost and regained the title twice. He won WWE's European Championship as well. Shawn was one of wrestling's biggest stars, and he knew how to entertain a crowd. One time Shawn even entered the ring by sliding down a cable from the ceiling.

Shawn worked to build up a bad-boy image. In 1997, he partnered with Triple H to form a group of heels called D-Generation X (DX). The group quickly became a fan favorite.

Shawn was a successful wrestler, but he struggled in his personal life. Wrestling was taking its toll on his body. His back was badly injured. He was also making unhealthy choices outside of the ring. At one point, he told a wrestling crowd, "I have to find my smile."

Shawn got the nickname "HBK" in the 1990s.

Shawn lost his title to Steve Austin at WrestleMania XIV.

Stepping Away

In March 1998, Shawn held the World Championship title for the third time. Then he suffered a tough loss to Stone Cold Steve Austin at WrestleMania. The toughest part of the defeat wasn't losing the belt. It was his back. Shawn had suffered a back injury months earlier. Now the pain was so bad that he couldn't move. Shawn left wrestling to treat his injuries. He thought he was done for good.

For the next four years, Shawn didn't wrestle. In 1999, he met and married Rebecca Curci. With her help, Shawn began to turn his life around. He started a training program in San Antonio called the Shawn Michaels Wrestling Academy. He even ran a small professional league called the Texas Wrestling Alliance.

Less Size, More Speed

Shawn is 6 feet, 1 inch (1.9 meters) tall and weighs 225 pounds (102 kilograms). That's not small for an average man, but it is for a wrestler. The Undertaker, for example, is 8 inches (20 centimeters) taller and 75 pounds (34 kilograms) heavier.

Shawn has used his small size well. He's speedier than most wrestlers. His size has also allowed him to do more high-flying moves.

Once, when wrestling against Vince McMahon, Shawn climbed a 30-foot (9-meter) ladder and leapt. McMahon was below, stuck inside a garbage can and lying on a table. Shawn landed squarely on McMahon. He dented the can and broke the table in half.

With Triple H's help, Shawn returned to WWE in 2002.

GETTING BETTER AND GETTING BACK

In 2000, Shawn and Rebecca had a son, Cameron. The birth of his son helped Shawn make better choices with his life. He began eating better and getting back into shape.

By summer 2002, Shawn felt healthy, fit, and happy. He was ready to get back in the ring. Shawn called his longtime friend Triple H and asked if the wrestler would face him in a match. That August, Triple H and Shawn squared off at SummerSlam. Shawn won the comeback match, and his career was reborn.

Among the Best Ever

Since his comeback, Shawn has fought impressive matches against legends such as Hulk Hogan. He has also battled younger stars like John Cena. While Shawn's high-flying moves are as dazzling as ever, he's changed in other ways. His jokes during WWE shows are much cleaner. He leaves the scene when other wrestlers are doing things Shawn considers inappropriate. He does this because of his children. Along with Cameron, Shawn has a daughter named Cheyenne, who was born in 2004. Shawn has said he doesn't want his kids to turn on the TV and see him doing something bad.

What his kids will see on TV is a great wrestler. WWE announcer Jim Ross has said that Shawn is one of the best wrestlers of all-time.

Shawn continues to be a fan favorite.

GLOSSARY ★ ★ ★ ★ ★ ★

babyface (BAY-bee-fayss) — a wrestler who acts as a hero in the ring

feud (FYOOD) — to argue and fight with another person or group of people

heel (HEEL) — a wrestler who acts as a villain in the ring

promoter (pruh-MOH-tur) — someone who helps with the growth or development of a wrestler's career

signature move (SIG-nuh-chur MOOV) — the move for which a wrestler is best known; this move is also called a finishing move.

tag team (TAG TEEM) — when two wrestlers partner together against other teams

READ MORE

Kaelberer, Angie Peterson. *Triple H.* Stars of Pro Wrestling. Mankato, Minn.: Capstone Press, 2010.

Shields, Brian, and Kevin Sullivan. *WWE Encyclopedia.* New York: DK Publishing, 2009.

 ## INTERNET SITES

FactHound offers a safe, fun way to find Internet sites related to this book. All of the sites on FactHound have been researched by our staff.

Here's all you do:

Visit *www.facthound.com*

FactHound will fetch the best sites for you!

INDEX ★ ★ ★ ★ ★ ★ ★